Amphibiana Amazing WATER FROGS

by Meish Goldish

Consultant: Dr. Kenneth L. Krysko
Senior Biological Scientist, Division of Herpetology
Florida Museum of Natural History, University of Florida

BEARPORT
PUBLISHING

New York, New York

Credits

Cover and Title Page, © Ryan M. Bolton/Shutterstock and Roze Petal/Shutterstock; TOC, © Brad Thompson/Shutterstock; 4, © Daniel Heuclin/NHPA/Photoshot; 5, © Daniel Heuclin/Biosphoto/Peter Arnold Inc.; 6T, © Martin Gabriel/NPL/Minden Pictures; 6C, © blickwinkel/Alamy; 6B, © Florian Moellers/age fotostock/SuperStock; 7T, © Johnny Jensen/Image Quest Marine; 7B, © Luis Castañeda/age fotostock/SuperStock; 8T, © Daniel Heuclin/NHPA/Photoshot; 8B, © Carl R. Sams/Peter Arnold, Inc./Alamy; 9, © Dante Fenolio/Photo Researchers, Inc.; 10T, © Studio Carlo Dani/Animals Animals Enterprises; 10B, © Ingo Arndt/Foto Natura/Minden Pictures; 11, © Pete Oxford/Minden Pictures; 12, © Dwight Kuhn Photography; 13L, © Betty & Nathan Cohen/Visuals Unlimited, Inc.; 13R, © Fritz Rauschenbach/Corbis; 14T, © Gary Meszaros/Visuals Unlimited, Inc.; 14B, © Michael Krabs/imagebroker/Alamy; 15, © Rolf Nussbaumer/NPL/Minden Pictures; 16, © David Brownell Photography; 17T, © Robert McGouey/Alamy; 17B, © D. R. Schrichte/SeaPics; 18T, © Edward R. Degginger/Bruce Coleman Inc./Photoshot; 18B, © Phil Degginger/Bruce Coleman Inc./Photoshot; 19, © Alvin E. Staffan/Photo Researchers, Inc.; 20, © Gary Meszaros/Visuals Unlimited, Inc.; 21T, © Dan Suzio/Photo Researchers, Inc.; 21B, © Breck P. Kent/Animals Animals Enterprises; 22T, © David Cavagnaro/DRK Photo; 22B, © Pete Oxford/Minden Pictures; Back Cover, © Brad Thompson/Shutterstock.

Publisher: Kenn Goin
Editorial Director: Adam Siegel
Creative Director: Spencer Brinker
Design: Debrah Kaiser
Photo Researcher: Picture Perfect Professionals, LLC

Library of Congress Cataloging-in-Publication Data

Goldish, Meish.
  Amazing water frogs / by Meish Goldish.
     p. cm. — (Amphibiana)
  Includes bibliographical references and index.
  ISBN-13: 978-1-936087-34-1 (library binding)
  ISBN-10: 1-936087-34-0 (library binding)
 1. Frogs—Juvenile literature. 2. Freshwater animals—Juvenile literature. I. Title.
  QL668.E2G637 2010
  597.8'9—dc22

2009040896

For more information, write to Bearport Publishing Company, Inc., 101 Fifth Avenue, Suite 6R, New York, New York 10003. Printed in the United States of America in North Mankato, Minnesota.

122009
090309CGD

10 9 8 7 6 5 4 3 2 1

Contents

A Giant Frog

In a rain forest in West Africa, hunters search the riverbank for food. The river's water level is lower than usual because of a **drought**, so it is easier for the hunters to spot their **prey**—a goliath frog.

Goliath frogs live in rivers in a small section of West Africa.

One frog may not seem like much of a meal, but this creature is different. The goliath frog is the biggest frog in the world. It grows to be more than one foot (.3 m) long. With its legs stretched out, the goliath frog can be almost three feet (.9 m) long. That's the same length as many skateboards!

A goliath frog can weigh up to seven pounds (3.2 kg). It is as heavy as some pet cats.

The Same but Different

It's not surprising that some frogs are found in rivers. After all, frogs are **amphibians**—animals that usually spend part of their lives in water and part on land. Toads, salamanders, and newts are also amphibians.

salamander

newt

toad

Not all frogs live in water for the same length of time, however. As adults, some kinds of frogs stay mostly on the ground. Others move into trees. Still others, such as the goliath frog, stay in water nearly all their lives. These frogs are called water frogs. They are also known as **aquatic frogs**.

◁ **The Zaire dwarf clawed frog is an aquatic frog.**

▽ **This tree frog is not aquatic. It spends most of its life on trees and other plants.**

Amphibians need water to keep their skin **moist** and their bodies cool. If their skin dries up or they become too hot, they will die.

Water Worlds

Aquatic frogs have many kinds of water homes. Goliath frogs live in fast-moving rivers. Green frogs stay in shallow ponds, springs, creeks, and brooks. Puddle frogs live in streams, marshes, and—of course—puddles.

Water frogs live in most parts of the world. These maps show where two kinds—the goliath frog and the American bullfrog—are found.

goliath frog

Africa

Indian Ocean

Atlantic Ocean

N W E S

Where goliath frogs live

American bullfrog

North America

Pacific Ocean

Atlantic Ocean

N W E S

Where American bullfrogs live

Many **species** of aquatic frogs live in places that are warm all year, such as tropical rain forests. Others live in colder parts of the world. To survive the winter, these aquatic frogs **hibernate**. They bury themselves in mud to keep from freezing. They stay there until the weather warms up in the spring.

Like all amphibians, water frogs are cold-blooded. That means their body temperature rises or drops with the temperature of their surroundings.

An American bullfrog hibernating

Going with the Flow

Since aquatic frogs spend most of their time in the water, their bodies are shaped in ways that make them excellent swimmers. Unlike many ground and tree frogs, water frogs have feet with **webbed toes** that act like paddles to help them swim. They also have long, strong back legs that push them through the water.

Like a duck, the African clawed frog has webbed toes to help it swim.

A close-up view of an ▷ African clawed frog's webbed toes

The skin of aquatic frogs helps the animals live in their wet homes, too. Tiny holes in the skin, called pores, are able to take in **oxygen** that is in the water. As a result, the animals are able to breathe underwater.

When frogs swim around a lot, they need more oxygen than the amount they can take in through their skin. To get extra oxygen, they rise to the surface of the water and gulp air into their **lungs**.

△ The Lake Titicaca frog has large folds of skin that allow it to take in lots of oxygen in the water.

Feeding Time

Aquatic frogs hunt other animals for food. They eat almost any kind of creature they find in or near the water where they live, including insects, worms, spiders, and small fish. Some frogs even eat other frogs!

Frogs don't chew their ▷ prey. Instead, they swallow them whole.

To catch their prey, many water frogs sit very still and wait for their victims to move in close enough for them to strike. Then some of these water frogs flick their sticky tongues out and pull the creatures into their mouths. Other water frogs have no tongues. They simply bite their victims or suck them into their mouths.

Some aquatic frogs have a lateral line that runs along their sides. This **organ** picks up **vibrations** and allows the frog to sense when other animals are moving in the water nearby.

lateral line on an African clawed frog

Frogs often leap out of the water to catch insects that are flying overhead.

Safety First

Water frogs are skillful hunters. Yet they need to be careful. Other animals that live near the frogs' watery homes are also out looking for food. Many of these **predators**, including large fish, birds, and snakes, want to catch and eat water frogs.

◁ This leopard frog was caught by a largemouth bass.

This snake is ▷ swallowing an American bullfrog.

Luckily, aquatic frogs have several ways to stay safe. They can hide in the water by swimming with just their eyes poking up above the water's surface. Frogs with a lateral line can also feel the movement of predators in the water.

When aquatic frogs sense danger, they dive down for safety and swim away. Sometimes they hide among water plants. If they're on land, they leap into the water. The big splash they make often scares off enemies.

It's easy for water frogs to spot enemies. Their eyes bulge out of their heads so that the frogs can see in all directions—even behind them.

△ Frogs often stay hidden by swimming mostly below the water. The color of their skin also helps them blend in with their surroundings.

Laying Eggs

In the spring, water frogs **mate**. Many male frogs call out to attract females. Each kind of frog makes a different sound. Females listen carefully to find frogs that are the same species as themselves.

A male bullfrog's throat blows up like a balloon when sounding its mating call.

After mating, the females lay their eggs in water. The eggs are covered with a sticky jelly rather than a hard shell. Aquatic frogs may lay hundreds or even thousands of eggs at a time. Most aquatic frogs don't guard their eggs, however. As a result, fish, snakes, and birds eat many of the eggs before they are ready to hatch.

This female bullfrog is laying eggs in a pond. She can lay up to 20,000 eggs at once.

A frog's eggs are ▷ covered with a sticky jelly that helps them cling to plants in the water.

Baby Frogs

A water frog's eggs hatch about a week after being laid. The baby frogs are called tadpoles. They look like tiny fish. They are born without legs but have a long tail for swimming. Like fish, tadpoles have **gills** on the sides of their heads. They use the gills to breathe in oxygen from the water.

Bullfrog tadpoles still in their eggs

gills

Bullfrog tadpoles hatching from eggs

Unlike adult frogs, tadpoles eat mostly small water plants. Tadpoles are unable to protect themselves, so many get eaten by fish, snakes, birds, and insects.

A bullfrog tadpole can grow to about six inches (15 cm) long.

Tadpoles of all frog species—even ground frogs and tree frogs—must stay in water to survive.

Big Changes

Several weeks after hatching, tadpoles start to go through big changes in the water. Scientists call what happens metamorphosis, which means a "change in form." The tadpoles grow legs, and their tails shorten until they disappear. In addition, their gills shrink and they grow lungs for breathing air.

This bullfrog tadpole has grown legs.

After about 12 weeks, the young of many species are no longer tadpoles. They're little frogs that will grow larger over time. Some crawl onto land to try out their new legs. However, like all aquatic frogs, they'll spend most of their lives right where they were born—in the water.

◁ Some kinds of young water frogs, such as the American bullfrog, come out of the water before their tails completely disappear.

Adult water frogs can live about 25 years.

Although many water frog species change from tadpoles to adults in a few months, it takes two or three years for American bullfrog tadpoles to become adults.

Water Frogs in Danger

Water frogs have been on Earth for millions of years. However, scientists fear that some species may now be in danger of becoming **extinct** due to diseases and changes in the **environment**.

Because water frogs take in air and water through their skin, they are especially sensitive to **pollution**. Also, as more ponds and streams are drained to make way for new buildings, more water frogs lose their homes and places to mate.

In some areas in the world, certain kinds of water frogs are already extinct. Here are two kinds that are currently in danger.

Western Leopard Frog

- This water frog got its name because its round, dark spots look like those on a leopard.
- Leopard frogs were once common in ponds, lakes, and streams in the western United States.
- Today, these frogs are very rare, due mainly to **pesticides** that farmers have sprayed on crops that grow near water—and that are deadly to leopard frogs.

Lake Titicaca Frog

- This frog is found only in Lake Titicaca, a huge body of water located in South America between Peru and Bolivia.
- Lake Titicaca frogs are declining in number because some people believe that the frogs can be used to make medicines. Other people enjoy eating them for food. As a result, as many as 150 frogs are killed each day.
- To help save the frogs, scientists have taken some of them out of their natural homes and placed them in **captivity**, where they can live safely and have young.

Glossary

amphibians (am-FIB-ee-uhnz) animals that usually spend part of their lives in water and part on land

aquatic frogs (uh-KWAT-ik FROGS) frogs that spend most of their adult lives in water

captivity (kap-TIV-uh-*tee*) places where animals live in which they are cared for by people, and which are not the animals' natural environments

drought (DROUT) a long period of time with little or no rain

environment (en-VYE-ruhn-muhnt) the area where an animal or plant lives, and all the things, such as weather, that affect that place

extinct (ek-STINGKT) when a kind of plant or animal has died out

gills (GILZ) the body parts of a water animal that are used for breathing

hibernate (HYE-bur-nayt) to spend the winter in a deep sleep to escape the cold

lungs (LUHNGZ) the body parts of an animal used for breathing air

mate (MAYT) to come together to produce young

moist (MOIST) slightly wet

organ (OR-guhn) a part of the body, such as the lungs or the heart, that does a particular job

oxygen (OK-suh-juhn) a colorless gas found in the air and water

pesticides (PESS-tuh-syedz) chemicals used to kill insects and other pests

pollution (puh-LOO-shuhn) harmful materials that damage the air, water, and soil

predators (PRED-uh-turz) animals that hunt other animals for food

prey (PRAY) an animal that is hunted for food

species (SPEE-sheez) groups that animals are divided into, according to similar characteristics; members of the same species can have offspring together

vibrations (vye-BRAY-shuhnz) quick back-and-forth shaking movements that can be felt

webbed toes (WEBD TOHZ) toes that are connected by a piece of skin

Index

Bibliography

Badger, David. *Frogs*. Stillwater, MN: Voyageur Press (2000).

Beltz, Ellin. *Frogs: Inside Their Remarkable World*. Buffalo, NY: Firefly Books (2005).

Showler, Dave. *Frogs and Toads*. New York: St. Martin's Press (2004).

Read More

Bishop, Nic. *Frogs*. New York: Scholastic (2008).

Moffett, Mark W. *Face to Face with Frogs*. Washington, D.C.: National Geographic (2008).

Morgan, Sally. *Amphibians*. Chicago: Raintree (2005).

Learn More Online

To learn more about water frogs, visit
www.bearportpublishing.com/Amphibiana

About the Author

Meish Goldish has written more than 200 books for children. He lives in Brooklyn, New York, where he likes to visit the Atlantic Ocean.